D1265937

AFRICAN-AMERICAN ARTISTS

CAROL ELLIS

TITLES IN THIS SERIES

AFRICAN-AMERICAN ARTISTS

CAROL ELLIS

MASON CREST
PHILADELPHIA

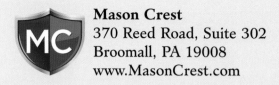

Mason Crest
370 Reed Road, Suite 302
Broomall, PA 19008
www.MasonCrest.com

Printed and bound in the United States of America.

CPSIA Compliance Information: Batch #MBC2012-2. For further information, contact Mason Crest at 1-866-MCP-Book.

First printing
1 3 5 7 9 8 6 4 2

Library of Congress Cataloging-in-Publication Data

Ellis, Carol, 1945-
African American artists / Carol Ellis.
pages cm — (Major black contributions from emancipation to civil rights)
Includes bibliographical references and index.
ISBN 978-1-4222-2372-7 (hc)
ISBN 978-1-4222-2385-7 (pb)
1. African American artists—Juvenile literature. I. Title.
N6538.N5E43 2012
704.03'96073—dc23

2011051945

Publisher's note: All quotations in this book are taken from original sources, and contain the spelling and grammatical inconsistencies of the original texts.

Picture credits: Associated Press: 51 (top); Fine Arts Museums of San Francisco: 24; Getty Images: 7, 41, 46; High Museum of Art: 53; Library of Congress: 8, 10, 14 (bottom), 27, 28, 34, 35, 36, 38, 39 (bottom), 55, 58; National Guard Heritage Series: 18; used under license from Shutterstock, Inc.: 51; Smithsonian American Art Museum: 3, 11, 13, 14 (top), 20, 23, 26, 31, 38 (top), 44; Wikimedia Commons: 16, 51 (bottom).

TABLE OF CONTENTS

INTRODUCTION

Dr. Marc Lamont Hill

It is impossible to tell the story of America without telling the story of Black Americans. From the struggle to end slavery, all the way to the election of the first Black president, the Black experience has been a window into America's own movement toward becoming a "more perfect union." Through the tragedies and triumphs of Blacks in America, we gain a more full understanding of our collective history and a richer appreciation of our collective journey. This book series, MAJOR BLACK CONTRIBUTIONS FROM EMANCIPATION TO CIVIL RIGHTS, spotlights that journey by showing the many ways that Black Americans have been a central part of our nation's development.

In this series, we are reminded that Blacks were not merely objects of history, swept up in the winds of social and political inevitability. Rather, since the end of legal slavery, Black men and women have actively fought for their own rights and freedoms. It is through their courageous efforts (along with the efforts of allies of all races) that Blacks are able to enjoy ever increasing levels of inclusion in American democracy. Through this series, we learn the names and stories of some of the most important contributors to our democracy.

But this series goes far beyond the story of slavery to freedom. The books in this series also demonstrate the various contributions of Black Americans to the nation's social, cultural, technological, and intellectual growth. While these books provide new and deeper insights into the lives and stories of familiar figures like Martin Luther King, Michael Jordan, and Oprah Winfrey, they also introduce readers to the contributions of countless heroes who have often been pushed to the margins of history. In reading this series, we are able to see that Blacks have been key contributors across every field of human endeavor.

Although this is a series about Black Americans, it is important and necessary reading for everyone. While readers of color will find enormous purpose and pride in uncovering the history of their ancestors, these books should also create similar sentiments among readers of all races and ethnicities. By understanding the rich and deep history of Blacks, a group often ignored or marginalized in history, we are reminded that everyone has a story. Everyone has a contribution. Everyone matters.

The insights of these books are necessary for creating deeper, richer, and more inclusive classrooms. More importantly, they remind us of the power and possibility of individuals of all races, places, and traditions. Such insights not only allow us to understand the past, but to create a more beautiful future.

ART GALLERY,
CENTENNIAL INTERNATIONAL EXHIBITION
1876.
FAIRMOUNT PARK   PHILADELPHIA.

View of the art gallery at the 1876 Centennial Exposition, held in Philadelphia. The Exposition helped to launch the careers of several talented African-American artists in the 19th century.

1

FOREVER FREE

Fireworks lit the sky. Mayors made speeches. Parades took place in small towns and big cities. The year was 1876. The United States was celebrating 100 years of independence. To make things even better, the country hosted a world's fair. It was called the Centennial Exposition. The fair took place in Philadelphia, Pennsylvania. Millions of people visited. They saw new inventions like the telephone and the calculator. They saw steam-powered drills and exotic plants. In one hall, they saw sculptures and paintings by artists from all over the world.

Painting number 54, "Under the Oaks," won the highest prize for an oil painting. It was a pastoral scene. It showed a herd of sheep gathered under a cluster of large oak trees. The painter was Edward Mitchell Bannister. When he read that his painting had won, he had to make sure it was true.

He rushed over to the hall. He told a friend what happened with the person in charge:

"I want to inquire concerning No. 54. Is it a prize winner?"

"What's that to you?" said he.

In an instant my blood was up; the looks that passed between him and others in the room were unmistakable. I was not an artist to them, simply an inquisitive colored man. Controlling myself, I said . . . "I am interested in the report that 'Under the Oaks' has received a prize. I painted the picture."

An explosion could not have made a more marked impression. Without hesitation he apologized to me, and soon everyone in the room was bowing and scraping to me.

Edward M. Bannister was the first African American to win a national prize for his art. He was born in Canada in 1828. He loved to draw and he was good at it. When he was a boy, he looked carefully at paintings that hung in the library. Then he copied them "on barn doors, fences and every place where drawings could be made."

To earn money, he became a cook on fishing boats. He learned to be an expert sailor. His trips often took him to Boston, Massachusetts. He decided to live there. In Boston, he worked as a barber. Cutting hair kept food on the table. It also helped pay for drawing classes and painting lessons.

Edward Bannister loved the countryside and the seaside. He could paint both of

Catalogue of artworks shows at the 1876 International Exhibition. When the judges learned Edward Bannister was African American, some wanted to reconsider their votes. However, the other artists insisted that Bannister deserved the top prize.

Two paintings by Edward M. Bannister, "Fisherman by Water" (1886) and "Driving Home the Cows" (1881), show the types of scenes he painted in Providence, Rhode Island.

them when he moved to Providence, Rhode Island. That is where he painted "Under the Oaks." One art critic called it "the greatest of its kind that we have seen by an American artist."

EDMONIA LEWIS

Another African-American artist, Edmonia Lewis, did not win a prize at the 1876 fair. But her sculpture drew some of the biggest crowds. It was carved in white marble. It weighed two tons. "The Death of Cleopatra" shows the Egyptian queen right after she died. She is still holding the poisonous snake that bit her.

People were shocked. No one had ever sculpted Cleopatra that way. But Edmonia Lewis did not do things the way everyone else did. Just the fact that she was a sculptor was unusual. At the time, sculpting was considered a "man's" art. Women did not carve huge pieces of art. But Edmonia Lewis did.

For another thing, Edmonia was an African American woman. They usually didn't go to college. They almost never sailed to Italy to make sculptures. Edmonia Lewis did both.

Edmonia Lewis was born around 1840. Her father was black. Her mother was Native American. Both parents died when she was very young. Later, her older brother sent her to Oberlin College. It was one of the few colleges in the United States that allowed women and African Americans to attend. She became good at drawing in college. Then she moved to Boston. She made clay medallions of the heads of famous people. She sold enough of them to pack her bags and sail to Rome, Italy.

SCULPTING

Rome was a great place for sculptors in the 1860s. It had statues they could study. It had plenty of marble to work with. Edmonia practiced her

"The Death of Cleopatra" did not go back to Rome. Edmonia Lewis showed it at a fair in Chicago, Illinois. Then she put it into storage. Things went wrong after that. The statue turned up in a saloon. Next it was moved to a racetrack. It was on the grave of a racehorse named Cleopatra. It stayed there for almost 100 years. The racetrack became a golf course. Golfers played around the sculpture. Then a big mail center was built on the land. "The Death of Cleopatra" wound up in a heavy equipment yard. A fireman saw it. He thought it was beautiful. He got his son's Boy Scout troop to clean and paint it. The head of a historical group read about it in the newspaper. He saw the statue. And he found the words "E. Lewis – Roma," carved on the base. The long-lost Cleopatra had been found. Today it is in the Smithsonian American Art Museum.

skills. She copied many of the statues. She also created small pieces of her own. She sold them to tourists and to people back in the United States. She made busts of famous men like Ulysses S. Grant and Abraham Lincoln.

One of the first sculptures she did in Rome is called "Forever Free." It shows a black man who has broken the chains of slavery. A black woman kneels by his side. She clasps her hands gratefully. Edmonia sculpted it to celebrate the Emancipation Proclamation of 1863.

In 1876, Edmonia Lewis shipped "The Death of Cleopatra" to Philadelphia. One person wrote that it was "the most remarkable piece of sculpture in the American section."

One of the best-known African-American artists of the 19th century was Henry Ossawa Tanner (1859–1937). He studied in Philadelphia under the American master of realism Thomas Eakins, then moved to Paris, Many of his paintings depict Biblical scenes, such as the one above, titled "And He Disappeared out of Their Sight" (1898), which depicts a scene from the Gospel of Luke in which the risen Jesus eats dinner with two of his disciples. The portrait of Tanner on the left was taken in the early 1930s.

No one knows exactly where Edmonia Lewis was born. No one is sure when she died. Someone wrote about her in 1909. She was still living in Rome. There is no record of her death. But her sculptures tell the story of an African American artist who dared to do things her own way.

A WORK OF ART

Jennie Smith was an art teacher. In 1886, she went to the Cotton Fair in Athens, Georgia. Later, she wrote about it. The fair was "on a much larger scale than an ordinary county fair, as there was a 'Wild West' show, and Cotton Weddings; and a circus, all at the same time." It was also the kind of fair where farmers showed off their crops. Who grew the biggest watermelon? Who made the best pickles? Whose cotton stalks were the tallest?

Jennie found something at the fair. It was more exciting to her than a gigantic watermelon or a tasty pickle. She discovered a work of art. "In one corner," she wrote, "there hung a quilt—which 'captured my eye.'"

The quilt was a patchwork quilt. It was divided into squares. The woman who made it had cut out pieces of fabric in the shapes of people and stars and animals. Then she had stitched the shapes onto the squares. Each square became a scene. They were scenes of Bible stories. There was Adam and Eve in the Garden of Eden. One scene showed the Last Supper. Another was of Christ being baptized.

Jennie Smith had seen many quilt patterns over the years. But she had never seen one that showed living creatures. It was original. Who had made this amazing quilt? Jennie had to find out. She went looking. "After much difficulty I found the owner, a negro woman, who lives in the country on a little farm," she wrote. The woman's name was Harriet Powers.

QUILTING ART

Harriet Powers was born into slavery in 1837. Many slave women made clothes and quilts for their owners and for themselves. Harriet probably learned to quilt while she was still a slave.

A lot had changed in the country between 1837 and 1886. The Civil

The "Bible Quilt" (1886)

The "Pictorial Quilt" (1898)

War between the northern and southern states broke out in 1861. In 1863, President Lincoln signed the Emancipation Proclamation. It freed slaves in many of the southern states. After the Civil War ended in 1865, the Thirteenth Amendment to the U.S. Constitution abolished slavery all over the United States.

Now it was 1886. Harriet Powers was 49 years old. She and her husband owned their own farm. They had several children. Harriet may have still sewed clothes and quilts for her family. But the quilt she took to the Cotton Fair was not one of them. It was there to be judged. It might win a prize. The fair was a place to exhibit her work for people to see and admire. Jennie Smith certainly admired it. She wanted to buy it, but "it was not for sale at any price."

A few years later, Harriet Powers sent a message to Jennie. Times were hard. She and her husband needed money. She was willing to sell the quilt. Jennie Smith bought it for five dollars.

MEANT TO BE ART

No one is sure how many quilts Harriet Powers created. Only two of them have survived. People call the second one the "Pictorial Quilt." It has scenes from the bible on it like the one Jennie Smith bought. It also has scenes that tell other stories. One panel shows a bitter cold night. It was so cold that people and animals froze in their tracks. There is a scene of falling stars and one of meteor showers. The biggest figure on the quilt is a hog named Betts. Betts was a local legend. According to Harriet, she was "the independent hog who ran 500 miles from Georgia to Virginia."

The "Pictorial Quilt" had many owners over the years. During the early 1900s, it belonged to a man named Charles Cuthbert Hall. He hung it on a wall like a painting. Even his little great-grandson knew it was "not meant to be on a bed, but meant to be art."

This painting shows the U.S. Army's 369th Infantry charging into battle in France during World War I. Horace Pippin was a member of the 369th, one of the army's most decorated regiments, and was badly wounded in battle.

2

AFTER THE WAR

Horace Pippin took the paintbrush in his disabled right hand. He used his "good" left hand to hold his right wrist. Then he slowly guided the brush across the canvas. He was painting a picture called "The End of the War: Starting Home."

The war was World War I. Horace Pippin had joined the U.S. army to help fight it. He was part of a volunteer black regiment. They were serving in France in 1918. As Horace ran across "no-man's-land," a bullet tore into his right shoulder. It destroyed bones, nerves and muscles. When Horace Pippin started home, he thought he would never be able to draw again.

LEARNING ON HIS OWN

Horace liked drawing better than almost anything. That got him in trouble in school. He would draw a sketch of the spelling words he was supposed to be learning—a dog, a stove, a dishpan. "And the results were," he said, "I would have to stay after school and finish my lesson the right way."

Pippin grew up poor. His family had no money to spare for paintbrushes or paint. No one even thought of drawing lessons. Horace copied a funny face in an advertisement. It won a prize—a box of crayons, some watercolors and two paintbrushes He taught himself to draw.

According to the Smithsonian American Art Museum, "Horace Pippin's 'Old Black Joe' (1943) is an interpretation of plantation life and the lot of African American slaves. Pennsylvanian Pippin derived this image and its title from Stephen Foster's Civil War-era ballad of the same name, conveying the sense of loss that also haunts the ballad's lyrics. Primarily self-taught, Pippin's engaging narrative style led to national acclaim."

Horace Pippin needed to earn money after the war. He took a lot of odd jobs. But something was missing. He wanted to draw. But how could he? His right arm was useless. He finally found a way. He used a white-hot fireplace poker to burn pictures into wood. Then he filled the burned-out images with paint. It was hard, slow work. But it "brought me back to my old self," he later said.

Horace Pippin's "old self" kept the shapes and colors of everything in his mind. He had many pictures he wanted to paint. Creating the burned wood pictures made his right arm and hand stronger. In time, he was able to use a paintbrush again.

With the help of his good hand, he began to paint on canvas. He painted more images of the war. He painted people from the past like Abraham Lincoln and John Brown, the White abolitionist. He painted images from his childhood—a Christmas breakfast, a group of young black men singing together on a street corner, a milkman's wagon.

"The pictures . . . come to me in my mind and if to me it is a worthwhile picture I paint it," he said. "I do over the picture several times in my mind and when I am ready to paint it I have all the details I need."

DISCOVERY

Horace Pippin lived in a small town in Pennsylvania. No one in the art world knew about him. But he decided to try to sell some of his paintings. The town barber put some in his window. So did the shoemaker. One day, an art critic was walking through town. He spotted Pippin's work. Suddenly, everything began to change.

First came an art show in town. Then the Museum of Modern Art in New York held a show. It was called *Masters of Popular Painting—Artists of the People*. Four of Horace Pippin's paintings were in the show. More shows followed. People began to buy Horace Pippin's works. He did not have to do odd jobs anymore. His wife did not have to wash other people's clothes.

Horace Pippin made more paintings. He did them faster. But he did not change his life. He stayed in Pennsylvania. He did not change his style. Some people thought he should take art classes. Horace disagreed. He had

his own ideas about how to paint. "Pictures just come to my mind," he said. "I think them out with my brain, and then I tell my heart to go ahead."

ON THE MOVE

Horace Pippin lived mostly in one place. But after World War I, many African Americans were on the move. Life was not easy for them. They were free. But they were not equal, especially in the south. White people looked down on them. Jobs were hard to get. They wanted a better life. Thousands of them left farms and small towns. They headed to big cities like Chicago, Washington D.C., and New York.

Augusta Savage was one of the many who moved. She was born in a small Florida town. The town's biggest business was making bricks. They used clay they mined from the soil. Augusta used the clay to sculpt figures of ducks, pigs and chickens. When she was about fifteen, the head of the county fair gave her a booth. Her farm animal sculptures were a major hit with the crowds.

Augusta wanted to become a professional sculptor. She wanted to take art classes. She left Florida in 1921. She arrived in New York City with about five dollars in her pocket.

LEARNING AND WORKING

Augusta Savage did not have enough money for classes. But she had plenty of talent. That talent got her into Cooper Union Art School. The sculpture program was supposed to last four years. Her teachers passed her through the first year's work in two weeks. She finished the second year's work in one month. Then she thought she would have to quit. She could not afford food or rent anymore. Her school voted to pay her living expenses.

After art school, Augusta worked in laundries to make ends meet. And she kept on modeling clay figures. One was the bust of a young boy from the streets of Harlem. Harlem is the area in New York City where Savage lived. She called the sculpture "Gamin." Art critics and the public loved it. She won a fellowship to study in Paris, France. Friends in Harlem held

The French word *gamin* means "street urchin," and the figure's wrinkled shirt and cap emphasize his impoverished appearance.

fund-raising parties. They helped pay for her travel and clothes. Black teachers in Florida collected money. Augusta left for Paris in 1929. She took classes at a good art school. She visited museums and cathedrals to see different types of sculpture.

Augusta came back to New York in 1931. By then, the Great Depression had hit the country like a hammer. Millions of people—black and white—were out of work. They stood in bread lines because they could not buy food.

TEACHING AND HELPING

Augusta Savage knew all about being poor. She had survived it many times. She earned some money by sculpting busts of famous black leaders. She also started the Savage Studio of Arts and Crafts in Harlem. Anyone could come who wanted to sculpt or draw or paint. But Augusta wanted kids who were in trouble just to come and hang out. She said "they ought to know there are black artists."

Augusta Savage did more than sculpt and teach. She helped other African American artists find work. Millions of people lost their jobs during the Great Depression. So President Franklin Roosevelt started a program called the Works Progress Administration. The WPA paid people to work on public building projects. It also hired artists. It paid them to paint

Aaron Douglas and the Harlem Renaissance

Harlem is a neighborhood in New York City. It is one of the places African Americans moved to when they left the south. During the 1920s, it became a place of ideas. Musicians, writers, and artists lived and worked in Harlem. They talked about their place in American life, and expressed ideas about their past and their future through their artistic works. Their creative work inspired people all over the country. This period of time became known as the Harlem Renaissance.

One aspect of the Harlem Renaissance was that African Americans took greater pride in their heritage and accomplishments. Some blacks believed that they could "uplift the race" and challenge racism through literature, art, music, and other forms of expression. As a result, white Americans took notice of black creative arts in a way that they never had before.

One of the most influential artists of the 1920s was Aaron Douglas (1899–1979). He was a painter. His work captured the excitement of the time. It was bold and new. His paintings inspired many other artists. He also illustrated books for other important figures of the Harlem Renaissance, including James Weldon Johnson, Countee Cullen, Alain Locke, and others. His artwork appeared in the NAACP's magazine *The Crisis*, as well as in popular magazines like *Harper's* and *Vanity Fair*.

By the 1930s, Douglas's artwork was being exhibited in galleries all over the country. Aaron Douglas has been called "the father of African-American art."

Aaron Douglas, "Aspiration" (1936)

murals on buildings. It paid them to do sculptures and paintings. The art was shown in galleries. It was loaned to schools and libraries. Augusta convinced the WPA to hire black artists as well as white.

Some of Augusta's friends thought she spent too much time teaching and helping other artists. They thought she should do more sculpting. Augusta did not agree. She said, "If I can inspire one of these youngsters to develop the talent I know they possess, then my monument will be their work. No one could ask for more than that."

Augusta Savage inspired many young African American artists. She helped many others find work as artists. One of them was Jacob Lawrence.

PAINTING STORIES

Jacob Lawrence was thirteen when he moved to Harlem with his mother. She was afraid he might wind up in a street gang. She sent him to an after-school art program at the library. He tried everything—painting, carving, making papier-mache masks. He painted Harlem street scenes on cardboard boxes. His teacher knew he had talent. He sent Jacob to Augusta Savage's studio. It was now called the Harlem Community Art Center. A few years later, Augusta helped him get hired by the WPA. "If Augusta Savage hadn't insisted on getting me onto the project, I don't think I would ever have become an artist," he said.

Jacob Lawrence knew he was an

> **= Did You Know? =**
>
> Jacob Lawrence wrote and drew the pictures for many children's books. In addition, some of his paintings were turned into picture books for children. Two of these books are *Harriet and the Promised Land* (1968) and *The Great Migration: An American Story* (1993).

artist. He just didn't think he could make a living as one. He thought art would always be his hobby, not his job. Now he could paint every day. He could get paid for it. He could experiment with different paints. He shared ideas with other African American artists at the WPA center. The other artists knew he was a great talent. They urged him to keep at it, and he did.

Jacob Lawrence often visited libraries and museums to learn more about black history, so he could depict events in his paintings. This 1960 painting titled "The Library" is believed to depict the 135th Street Library in Harlem, New York, during the 1920s. An expert at the Smithsonian American Art Museum notes, "Everybody appears absorbed in their books, and the standing figure in the front looking at African art may represent the artist as a young man, delving deeper into his heritage." The 135th Street Library still exists; today it is a world-renowned research library known as the Schomburg Center for Research in Black Culture.

THE HISTORY PAINTER

Jacob Lawrence painted in bold patterns and bright colors. It looked very modern. He also read a lot about African-American history. He wanted to

This portrait of Jacob Lawrence (1917–2000) was taken in the early 1940s.

tell some of that history through his paintings. But he needed more than one painting to do it. Instead of a single painting, he made panels of paintings. He painted 31 panels to tell the story of Harriet Tubman. She was famous for helping slaves escape to freedom through the Underground Railroad.

The Migration of the Negro has sixty panels. The paintings tell the story of southern blacks who moved north. They wanted a better life. They wanted more freedom. Some panels show African Americans before they moved. They are working in the fields. Or they are reading a letter from relatives who have already gone north. Another panel shows a train station. It has signs for big cities like Chicago, New York, and St. Louis. Other panels paint pictures of their new lives. They live in apartment buildings. They work in steel mills instead of cotton fields. Sometimes life is better. Sometimes it is not.

In 1941, Jacob Lawrence became the first African American artist whose work was shown at a "white" gallery. He was 24 years old. When he was older, he began to teach. But he never stopped painting.

This photo by Gordon Parks, taken in 1942, would become a symbol of the way African Americans were treated before the Civil Rights era.

3

THE IMAGE MAKERS

African American artists came from different backgrounds. They had different experiences. Some went to college. Some never finished high school. But in America during the 1940s and 1950s, many white people did not see blacks as individuals. To them, they were all alike—and they were second-class citizens.

Many African Americans used their art to help change that image.

PATTI-JO 'N GINGER

Patti-Jo is a five-year-old girl. She has a quick mind and a sharp tongue. Her grown-up sister, Ginger, is beautiful. She wears the latest fashions. But she leaves all the talking to Patti-Jo. And Patti-Jo has plenty to say about everything—from clothes to politics to race.

Patti-Jo 'n Ginger was a comic strip. It ran in newspapers during the 1940s and 1950s. The artist who created it was Jackie Ormes. She was one of the first black female cartoonists in the United States.

Jackie Ormes was born in Pennsylvania. Later she lived in Chicago, Illinois. She created three comic strips. *Torchy, Dixie to Harlem* was the story of Torchy Brown. She was a young black woman from the south who moved to New York.

Patti-Jo 'n Ginger featured the quick-witted little girl and her older sister. *Torchy Heartbeats* was a romantic adventure.

The three comic strips ran in the funny pages of major African American newspapers. Ormes's characters often made statements about the segregation of blacks and the politics of the United States. But they did it with a lot of humor. The comic strips also dealt with funny, everyday situations.

A DIFFERENT IMAGE

In *Torchy, Dixie to Harlem*, Torchy is at the train station. She's going to New York. One arrow points to the train car for whites. Another arrow points to the car for blacks. Torchy decides to pretend she can't read. Then she boards the car for whites.

Patti-Jo 'n Ginger live in a modern apartment. It has beautiful rugs, lamps and furniture. And Ginger looks like she stepped out of a fashion magazine.

In *Torchy Heartbeats*, Torchy travels to foreign countries and stays in posh resorts.

The three comic strips showed African Americans going to college and art galleries and the theatre. They showed black women who were smart and beautiful. This was not the image many white people had of African Americans. It was not even the way some blacks saw themselves. Jackie Ormes's comic strip art drew a different picture for everyone.

=== Did You Know? ===

Jackie Ormes turned one of her cartoon characters, Patti-Jo, into a doll in the late 1940s. The Patti-Jo doll became very popular at the time. Today it is a favorite of doll collectors.

THE BIG PICTURE

Jackie Ormes drew comic strips. John T. Biggers painted walls. By the time he finished, he had painted walls in Virginia, Pennsylvania and Texas. But John Biggers was not painting graffiti. He was painting murals.

John Biggers was born in North Carolina. His father was a preacher. He was also a schoolteacher and a farmer. After John's father died, his mother had to support seven children. She cooked for white families. John always liked to draw, paint and sculpt. He and his older brother once made a scale model of their town. They carved houses from clay. They used moss for the grass.

But John did not plan to be an artist. He paid his way through high school by working on the school's heating and plumbing. Then he went to the Hampton Institute. It was an African American college in Virginia. Students learned to be teachers there. Or they got training in jobs like plumbing. That's what John Biggers had decided to study. But the college offered art classes, so he took one. It instantly "changed my life—and my goals," he said. "I began my career as an artist and teacher."

"Shotgun, Third Ward #1" is a 1966 painting by John T. Biggers (1924–2001).

PAINTINGS ON THE WALL

"My murals have been the central focus of my life as an artist. From my earliest artistic beginnings at the Hampton Institute, I have told stories about life through my paintings on the wall."

Many of John Biggers's murals told a story of black people in the south. It was a story of African Americans picking cotton, fishing, and cooking. The women in his murals did not wear high heels and fancy dresses. They were poor. They looked tired.

Then people looked at the paintings closely. And they saw another picture. African American women and men did not let their troubles beat them. They worked hard. They celebrated a good harvest. They cooked or made quilts together. They went to church. They took care of their children.

With his murals, John Biggers gave many African Americans pride in themselves.

THE ART OF TEACHING

John Biggers arrived at Texas State University in 1949. He had been hired to help start an art department. It was not easy. TSU was a black college in Houston, Texas. Most of the teachers did not think black students wanted to know about art. At first, there was not even a good place for them to paint. They were supposed to learn how by reading about it.

John Biggers solved that problem: He told his students to saw off the arms and backs of the classroom chairs. Now they had stools they could stand or sit on. Next he had them paint the classroom walls gray. Then he gave them an assignment: Paint murals on the walls. He told them not to worry about the "right" way to paint. He told them to think about their feelings. He told them to think about how they grew up. He asked them to think about their history. Then he said to paint them.

The art department at TSU began to grow. Houston newspapers wrote about it. They also wrote about John Biggers. He painted murals on many buildings in the city. He did smaller paintings that won prizes. He won a fellowship to go to West Africa. He saw people working the fields, fishing and sewing. It reminded him of the lives of African Americans.

When he came back to Texas, John Biggers put his African drawings into a book. And he kept teaching for many years. As a teacher, John Biggers showed his students "how their brushes can make paint tell stories."

LIFE IN PICTURES

The year was 1937. Gordon Parks was a waiter on a Pullman train. He looked at a magazine a passenger had left behind. The photographs showed migrant workers. They were picking vegetables and fruits in the fields. Migrant workers moved all over the country to work on big farms. They got paid a few cents an hour. They lived in shacks or tents. If they got sick, they lost their jobs. They were out of food. They were out of luck. In the south, many of them were African American.

The photos upset Gordon Parks. They also made him think. "I saw that the camera could be a weapon against poverty, against racism, against all sorts of social wrongs," he told an interviewer in 1999. "I knew at that point I had to have a camera."

Gordon Parks was born in 1912. His mother died when he was a teenager. Soon after that, he was on his own in Minnesota. He started high school, but he did not finish. He needed to earn money. He had never taken piano lessons. He taught himself to play so he could get paid. He sang with a big band. He worked as a busboy in diners. He even played semi-pro basketball. And he worked as a waiter on trains.

Gordon Parks finally bought his first camera at a second-hand shop. He paid $7.50 for it. Then he started taking pictures of everything—people, pets, parks and buildings. He took fashion pictures for a clothing store in Chicago. He took photos of Chicago's black ghetto. He started to get jobs taking photos. His most famous photo was of a black cleaning woman. Her name was Ella Watson. She stood in front of the American flag. She held a mop in one hand. In the other hand, she held a broom. (This photo, which

The Many Works of Gordon Parks

Gordon Parks (1912–2006) was a busy artist. He did much more than take photographs. He wrote books. He wrote poetry. He wrote music for orchestras. He wrote and played jazz and blues music. He even wrote the music for *Martin*, a ballet about Martin Luther King.

He was not just the first black photographer at *Life* magazine. He was the first black artist to produce and direct a major Hollywood film. It is called *The Learning Tree*, and was finished in 1969. He also directed two popular action films, *Shaft* and *Shaft's Big Score*.

Gordon Parks knew what it was like to be African American. He had been turned away from stores and restaurants because he was black. But he did not give up. He had confidence in himself. "I just forgot I was black and walked in and asked for a job," he said.

Gordon Parks in his Washington, D.C., office during the 1940s.

is titled "American Gothic" after a famous painting, appears on page 28.)

PICTURES IN LIFE

1948, Gordon Parks got a job at *Life* magazine. It was the most popular picture magazine of the time. Parks was the first African American to work on the magazine's staff. He was a photographer and writer. He worked there for many years. He took photos of movie stars and models. He photographed famous people like Muhammad Ali and Malcolm X.

Three boys who live in Harlem, photographed by Gordon Parks during the 1940s.

But Gordon Parks also took pictures of people who were not famous. He took photos of poor people, black and white. He took photos of a youth gang in Harlem. He photographed a young boy who lived in the slums of Brazil. The boy was very poor and very sick. Parks wrote his story and showed his life in photos. *Life*'s readers sent $30,000 to help the boy.

Gordon Parks's photos made him famous. They also got people to think. Not everyone was rich or famous. Gordon Parks got readers to sit up and take notice of the people who weren't.

The ceramic tile artwork titled ''Family'' (1986) was the final work by the great African American artist Romare Bearden (1911–1988). It was inspired by his childhood in North Carolina. "Family" is located just inside the entrance to a federal government building in the Jamaica neighborhood of New York.

4

CHANGING TIMES

The date was August 28, 1963. Hundreds of thousands of people gathered in Washington D.C. They were part of The March on Washington for Jobs and Freedom. They heard Dr. Martin Luther King Jr. give his famous "I Have A Dream" speech. He dreamed of a world where blacks and whites would be equal.

Many schools were still segregated in 1963. Many restaurants would not serve blacks. In some places, blacks had to pay a tax to vote. African Americans wanted equality. They wanted civil rights.

African American artists reacted to the Civil Rights Movement in different ways. A group of black artists met in New York to talk about it. All of them wanted equal rights. Should they use their art to protest? Or should art be kept apart from politics?

A BRIDGE BETWEEN PAST AND PRESENT

One of the artists at the meeting was Romare Bearden. He was born in North Carolina. He grew up in New York during the Harlem Renaissance. Musicians, writers and artists often visited his parents. When he was a teenager, he met the sculptor Augusta Savage. She was "a flesh and blood

Black Colleges Support Art

Black colleges played a big part in helping African American artists. They hired them as teachers. They showed their paintings and sculptures. Schools like Howard University, Hampton Institute, and Fisk University gave African-American artists a place to work and to be seen.

During the 1960s and 1970s, African American artists wanted equal rights as human beings. They also wanted equal treatment as artists. They urged important museums to include black artists in their shows. In 1968, The Museum of Modern Art in New York planned a show to honor Dr. Martin Luther King Jr. Not a single black artist's work was going to be part of it. African American artists protested. The museum decided to show the work of black artists.

By the 1980s, many "white" galleries and museums were showing the work of black artists. African Americans also opened their own galleries and museums. Some were in black districts of a city. Some were in white districts. African American art and artists were becoming part of the picture of America.

An art class at the Hampton Institute in Virginia, circa 1900. The students are learning to work with clay.

"Bopping at Birdland (Stomp Time)," painted in 1979, is one of the many colorful paintings in Romare Bearden's "Jazz Series." Another in the series, "Empress of the Blues" (1974), appears on page 3 of this book.

artist with a studio which we were welcome to use as a workshop, or even just to hang out in."

After college, Romare Bearden became a social worker in New York. But he also painted. By the time he met with the other artists in 1963, he was a well-known artist. His paintings were shown in art galleries and museums. Many of them showed scenes of African Americans in North Carolina. His grandparents had a boarding house in Pennsylvania. He spent a lot of time there and painted the steel mills and train stations.

Romare Bearden

Romare Bearden wanted equal right for African Americans. But he did not paint protest images. In fact, he did not use paint. He used photos he had taken. He cut pictures from magazines and posters. Then he made a collage by pasting them onto canvas.

Some of the photos were from the past. Some were of the present. He mixed images of farm life with modern street scenes in Harlem. Romare Bearden used collages to show the hopes and struggles of blacks in America.

WAVING THE FLAG

Many artists used images of the American flag in their work. It was a symbol of their country. Many of them had fought for the country in both world wars. But they were still not accepted.

"The Flag is Bleeding #2" shows an African American woman standing behind the flag. Its white stars almost hide her face. Her hands rest on the shoulders of two children in front of the flag. Blood drips from the flag's red stripes to the bottom of the painting. The artist was Faith Ringgold.

Faith Ringgold was born in Harlem, New York in 1930. She studied art at the City College of New York. During the 1960s, she did a series of paintings called The American People. "The Flag is Bleeding #2" was one of them. Some of the paintings were of blacks. Some were of whites. Many showed them together. Many were of women, black and white. Faith Ringgold wanted equal rights for everyone.

CHANGING STYLES

Faith Ringgold grew up knowing how to use a needle and thread. Her mother was a dressmaker and a fashion designer. Her great-great grandmother was a slave. She made quilts for her white masters. Faith put painting and sewing together. She came up with a different style of art. At first she made soft sculptures. She stuffed fabric with foam rubber. She painted and decorated the outside. Then she started making quilts—and painting them. Finally, she began writing stories on the outside borders of the

Faith Ringgold turned her story quilt "Tar Beach" into a children's book. She has written and drawn the pictures for many other children's books such as *Aunt Harriet's Underground Railroad in the Sky*, *Dinner at Aunt Connie's House*, *Cassie's Word Quilt*, *Counting to Tar Beach*, and *The Invisible Princess*.

quilts. One of those story quilts was called "Tar Beach." It tells the story of a little girl named Cassie Louise Lightfoot and her family hanging out on the rooftop on a hot summer night.

Many people believed that making quilts was "women's work." Like Harriet Powers, Faith Ringgold turned it into art.

> **— Did You Know? —**
>
> Roofs of apartment buildings were often covered with tar. People would go up to the roof in the summertime to keep cool. It was like going to the beach. So they called the roof "tar beach."

NEW ART

In the 1970s, graffiti began to appear on the sides of buildings in New York. The tag was SAMO. For awhile, no one knew who SAMO was. But then the spray-painter painted his last bit of graffiti: *Samo is Dead*. But he was not dead. His name was Jean-Michel Basquiat. He was about to become famous.

Jean-Michel Basquiat was born in Brooklyn, New York, in 1960. His father was from Haiti. His mother was Puerto Rican. She encouraged Jean-Michel to draw and paint. She took him to museums around the city. He was even a junior member of the Brooklyn Museum. Then Jean-Michel's parents divorced. He ran away from home when he was a teenager. He lived with friends. That's when he and a friend began spray-painting.

THE GRAFFITI MOVEMENT

Today people try to clean up graffiti as fast as they can. But graffiti was something new in the 1970s. Many people thought it was artistic. A lot of New Yorkers noticed Basquiat's graffiti. Newspapers wrote stories about it. SAMO was a mystery.

Then Jean-Michel and his friend had an argument. SAMO "died." After that, Jean-Michel dropped out of high school. He lived on the streets. He begged for money. He sold hand-painted postcards and T-shirts. He was

eighteen years old.

Jean-Michel Basquiat did not stay homeless for long. He joined a punk-rock band. He got a part in a movie. Somehow he kept creating his art. It was not on buildings anymore. It was on canvas. Basquiat hung out in SoHo. It is a part of New York City with a lot of art galleries. Jean-Michel was not afraid to walk right in and show his artwork.

> ## = Did You Know? =
>
> Collectors of modern art pay a lot of money for Jean-Michel Basquiat's paintings. In 2007, one of his paintings sold for more than $14 million .

FAME

Basquiat mixed things up in his work. He used paint. He wrote words and doodles. He copied images of junk food and cartoons. He used his art to say things about pop culture, politics and black history. It was different. It was new. It did not take long for Jean-Michel Basquiat to become famous. He had gallery shows. He had museum exhibits. His picture was on the cover of a magazine. Was his work pop art? Was it punk art? No one could agree. But most people agreed that he had talent. At first, his art looked like he just slapped things together. But he had an artist's eye. He had an artist's skill. He knew how to create an image that would last.

Jean-Michel Basquiat's images have lasted much longer than he did. He was twenty-eight years old when he died.

A WORLD OF COLOR

Jean-Michel Basquiat was born in 1960. That same year, Alma Thomas retired from teaching. She had been a teacher for about 35 years. Now she could paint all the time. Alma Thomas was born in 1891. She was old enough to be Basquiat's great-grandmother. But her art was as fresh and new as his.

Alma Thomas was born in Georgia. Her family moved to Washington D.C. when she was eleven. Alma loved gardens and colorful flowers. Those

The colorful abstract style of Alma Thomas (1891–1978) can be seen in "Fall Begins" (1976). In 2009, First Lady Michelle Obama chose several of Thomas's artworks to hang in the White House during the presidency of Barack Obama.

colors would show up in her paintings one day. But first, she became a teacher. She taught arts and crafts in kindergarten for six years. Then she became an art teacher in a junior high school. During the summers, she took art classes. She visited museums to study the paintings of famous artists. And she created her own art.

Her paintings looked "natural" at first. A flower looked like a flower. A pear was a pear. Then the paintings slowly began to change. Alma Thomas had studied many painters of modern art. Some were called abstract painters. They did not paint things the way they looked in the real world. Alma Thomas tried this in her own work. Then she took it a step further.

THE ART OF COLOR

One group of modern artists was called the Color Field group. They painted only in colors. They organized those colors into circles and stripes on the canvas. Alma Thomas loved color. She started covering her canvas with tiny shapes of bright color. She used the colors of flowers like cherry blossoms. She used the colors of leaves in the fall. She told someone she tried to paint as if she were looking down from an airplane: "You streak through the clouds so fast you don't know whether the flower below is a violet or what. You see only streaks of color."

When Alma Thomas retired from teaching, her "streaks of color" had been shown in many galleries and museums. She was admired and famous.

Alma Thomas was African American. She joined in Martin Luther King's March on Washington. She worked in community programs to help children see the work of African American artists. But she did not paint "black art" or black subjects. She was an artist first. She used to say "We artists are put on God's good earth to create. Some of us may be black, but that's not the important thing. The important thing is for us to create."

> === Did You Know? ===
>
> Alma Thomas was the first African American woman to have a solo exhibit at the Whitney Museum of American Art in New York.

The noted African-American sculptor Richard Hunt (b. 1935) grinds and polishes a metal sculpture at his studio in Chicago.

5

METAL, PAPER, AND COMPUTERS

In Chicago, Illinois, you do not have visit a museum to see a work of art by Richard Hunt. One is in a public library. Another is outside an office building. There are more than 30 of them. "You kind of bump into them all the time," said a Richard Hunt fan.

Richard Hunt creates sculptures. He makes small ones that are shown in museums and galleries. But he also makes very large ones. They are meant to be outdoors. They are public sculptures. And you won't see them only in Illinois. You can find them in Michigan, Georgia, and Tennessee. You can see them on college campuses. Outdoor art makes a city look good. It makes the people who live there feel good. It is fun to "bump into" a sculpture in the park or outside a library. Many cities use outdoor art today. And a lot of them ask Richard Hunt to create it.

THE PUBLIC ARTIST

Richard Hunt was born in Chicago in 1935. He went to college at the Art Institute of Chicago. That is where he studied sculpture. He served in the Army for two years. Then he kept sculpting. His work was shown in art fairs and small galleries.

In 1967, he was hired to create a very large sculpture. He did not have room to make it in his studio. So he worked on it in a metal shop. He said it was the start of his second career—being a public artist.

Richard Hunt's public sculptures get rained on. Snow and ice cover them. Wind whips around them. He makes his sculptures out of steel and other metals. He makes them to last.

DRAWING IN SPACE

Hunt's metal sculptures are abstract. They give the idea of an object. They do not make it look real. Many people see images of wings, birds and airplanes in his work.

Making large outdoor sculptures is different from modeling something that sits on a shelf. Richard Hunt has to think about the buildings that are nearby. He thinks about how much room he has. Hunt must imagine how his sculpture will look to someone walking by. Richard Hunt "draws in space."

DRAWING ON PAPER

Richard Hunt draws in space. Other artists use paper and pen. Jerry Craft and Aaron McGruder have different backgrounds. They have different ideas about being black. But both of them are artists who draw comic strips.

Jerry Craft grew up in New York City. He always liked to draw. But after he finished college, he got a job writing advertisements. Then the company went out of business. He needed to work. He decided to start drawing again. He had dreams of being the next great *Spiderman* artist for Marvel Comics.

Jerry Craft sold his first comic strip in 1987. *The Outside View* was about a group of teenage friends. They were black, white and Hispanic. Craft called it a "rainbow coalition." Then, in 1990, he decided to make major changes to the strip. He got rid of some characters. He added others. He called the new strip *Mama's Boyz*.

MAMA'S BOYZ

Mama's Boyz tells the story of
Pauline Porter. Pauline has two
teenage sons named Tyrell and
Yusuf. It is a story about family
and friends and getting along in
life. Problems are never too hard
to overcome. It is cheerful and
funny, even when it talks about
race or politics.

In 1997, Kings Features
Weekly picked up *Mama's Boyz*.
Kings is a company that sends cartoons to newspapers around the world.
Pauline, Tyrell and Yusuf were a big hit.

= Did You Know? =

Jerry Craft has diabetes. It is a dis-
ease that affects millions of people.
There is no cure. But it can be
controlled. The *Mama's Boyz*
characters have acted as national
spokescharacters for the American
Diabetes Association's African-
American Program.

OUT IN THE BOONDOCKS

Huey and Riley Freeman are brothers. Huey is ten years old. Riley is eight.
They used to live in Chicago. Then they moved with their Granddad to a
town in the suburbs. Huey calls it the boondocks.

Huey wants to change the world. He has a lot of things to say about politics and government. Most of them are not good things. Riley likes gangs-
ta rap. Granddad does not approve of any of their ideas.

The new town is quiet. The Freeman brothers stir things up.

The *Boondocks* comic strip stirred things up too.

AARON MCGRUDER

Aaron McGruder was born in Chicago in 1974. When he was very young,
his family moved to a suburban town. He loved the comics. *Peanuts* and
Doonesbury were two of his favorites. He also liked movies and television
programs made by a group of British comedians who called themselves
Monty Python. The comics and the films used humor to talk about serious
things like race and politics.

A daily *Boondocks* cartoon from 2005, at the height of the strip's popularity.

Aaron went to college at the University of Maryland. That's where he created his first *Boondocks* strip. At first, he put it online for people to read. Then the college newspaper needed a new comic strip. It began to run *The Boondocks*. It became a big hit on campus. Then a company that sells comic strips to newspapers bought the strip. In 1998, *The Boondocks* began running in about 160 newspapers around the country.

Many people loved the comic strip. Almost as many people hated it. Some thought it was funny. Others said it was hateful. Not everyone who loved it was black. And not everyone who hated it was white. Aaron McGruder's comic strip characters did not mince words about anybody, black or white. They criticized black musicians and white politicians. They criticized African-American actors and white millionaires. Some newspapers did not think *The Boondocks* belonged on the funny pages. A few of them put it on their opinion page.

But the comic strip kept running. It was very popular. By 1999, the strip was running in about 200 newspapers. By 2005, *The Boondocks* was appearing in almost 300 newspapers. That year, *The Boondocks*

Aaron McGruder

was made into an animated cartoon show for television. However, the pressure of creating both a daily comic strip and a television show led McGruder to stop publishing the comic in 2006. The television show still airs, however, and continues to stir things up.

DRAWING WITHOUT PAPER

Angela Perkins does not use paper or paint to create art. She uses a computer. She might start with the photograph of a face. With the computer, she can change the light. She can add shadows. She can add patterns that might look like African cloth. The face is still there, but it has changed. Angela Perkins has turned it into a new piece of art.

After college, Angela became a graphic designer. She got interested in computer graphics when she was studying at the Massachusetts Institute of Technology. She loved the light and the colors on the computer screen. She began using the computer to make art. For her, it was "as magical as using a brush, [or] crayon or...crafting."

Did You Know?

Radcliffe Bailey's art is called mixed media. Mixed media artists use two or more materials in their work. The different materials could be as "simple" as oil paint and chalk. Or artists can add pages from magazines and newspapers to their paintings. Many mixed media artists use letters, decals and photographs. Some artists combine them all.

PAST AND FUTURE

Radcliffe Bailey was born in 1968. He grew up and went to college in Georgia. He spent a lot of time with his grandparents when he was young. He learned what life was like for African Americans in the past. His grandmother gave him photographs. Many of the photos were taken during the Civil War. Today, some of those photos appear in Radcliffe Bailey's art. (A photo of Radcliffe Bailey discussing one of works in an art gallery appears on page 7 of this book.)

Sometimes Bailey paints on canvas. Sometimes he paints on wood. The

Radcliffe Bailey's "Windward Coast" was exhibited as part of his 2011-12 show "Memory as Medicine" at the High Museum of Art in San Francisco. Like several of the artist's other works, it refers to the transatlantic passage of African slaves to America between the 16th and 19th centuries.

paint is thick and bright. But he uses more than paint. He often uses pieces of metal or wood that he has found. Or he might use small signs or letters. Sometimes he combines them all.

And then there are the photographs. Radcliffe Bailey is African American. He uses his grandmother's photographs to help tell the story of the past. But the found objects and bright paint make his work part of the present and the future. "I'm like free jazz," he said. "I'm not concerned about where I'm going, just as long as I'm moving forward and documenting life."

CHAPTER NOTES

p. 10:   "I want to inquire . . ." Romare Bearden and Harry Henderson, *A History of African-American Artists from 1792 to the Present* (New York: Pantheon, 1993), p. 45.

p. 10:   "on barn doors, fences . . ." Ibid., p. 41.

p. 13:   "the most remarkable piece . . ." Stephen May, "The Object at Hand," *Smithsonian Magazine* (September 1996). http://www.smithsonian-mag.com/arts-culture/object_sep96.html?c=y&page=1

p. 15:   "on a much larger scale . . ." National Museum of American History, "Harriet Powers's 'Bible Quilt.'" http://americanhistory.si.edu/collections/object.cfm?key=35&objkey=7233&gkey=169

p. 15:   "In one corner . . ." Ibid.

p. 15:   "After much difficulty . . ." Ibid.

p. 16:   "it was not for sale . . ." Ibid.

p. 17:   "the independent hog . . ." Mary E. Lyons, *Stitching Stars: The Quilts of Harriet Powers* (New York: Aladdin, 1997), p. 24.

p. 17:   "not meant to be on a bed . . ." Kyra E. Hicks, *This I Accomplish: Harriet Powers' Bible Quilt and Other Pieces* (Arlington, VA: Black Threads Press, 2009), p. 180.

p. 19:   "And the results were . . ." Bearden and Henderson, *A History of African-American Artists*, p. 357.

p. 20:   "Horace Pippin's 'Old Black Joe' . . ." Smithsonian American Art Museum, "Touring Exhibition Celebrates African American Art," (February 28, 2003). http://americanart.si.edu/pr/library/2003/02/masters/

p. 20:   "brought me back . . ." Bearden and Henderson, *A History of African-American Artists*, p. 359.

p. 21:   "The pictures . . . come to me . . ." National Gallery of Art, "Meet Horace Pippin (1888–1946)." http://www.nga.gov/education/classroom/counting_on_art/bio_pippin.shtm

p. 22:   "Pictures just come to my mind..." Stephen May, "Horace Pippin's Art Finds the Grandeur in Unheralded Lives," *Smithsonian Magazine* (June 1994). http://www.smithsonianmag.com

p. 23:   "they ought to know . . ." Bearden and Henderson, *A History of African-American Artists*, p. 173.

p. 24:   "father of African-American art." Barbara La Blanc, "Aaron Douglas: Father of African-American Art," in *Contemporary Black Biography: Profiles from the International Black Community*, Vol. 7 (San Diego: Gale, 1994), p. 66.

p. 25:   "If I can inspire . . ." Bearden and Henderson, *A History of African-American Artists*, p. 176.

Jacob Lawrence gives a demonstration to students at the Abraham Lincoln School in Brooklyn, New York.

p. 25:   "If Augusta Savage hadn't . . ." Ibid., p. 297.

p. 26:   "Everybody appears absorbed . . ." Smithsonian American Art
            Museum, "The Library by Jacob Lawrence."
            http://americanart.si.edu/collections/search/artwork/?id=14376

p. 31:   "changed my life—and my goals. . . ." Bearden and Henderson, *A
            History of African-American Artists*, p. 430.

p. 32:   "My murals have been . . ." James Prigoff and Robin J. Dunitz, *Walls
            of Heritage, Walls of Pride: African-American Murals* (Bristol, UK:
            Pomegranate Books, 2000), p. 19.

p. 33:   "how their brushes can . . ." University of Houston, "John Biggers."
            http://atlantis.coe.uh.edu/biggers/legacy.htm

p. 33:   "I saw that the camera . . ." Andy Grundberg, "Gordon Parks, a
            Master of the Camera, Dies at 93," *New York Times* (March 8, 2006).
            http://www.nytimes.com/2006/03/08/arts/design/08parks.
            html?pagewanted=all

p. 34:   "I just forgot I was black . . ." Ibid.

p. 37:   "a flesh and blood artist . . ." National Gallery of Art, "The Art of
            Romare Bearden, a Resource for Teachers." http://www.nga.gov/edu-
            cation/classroom/bearden/bio2.shtm

p. 45:   "You streak through the clouds . . ." Bearden and Henderson, *A
            History of African-American Artists*, p. 451.

p. 45:   "We artists are put . . ." Ibid., p. 453.

p. 47:   "You kind of bump . . ." Jan Garden Castro, "Richard Hunt: Freeing
            the Human Soul," *Sculpture* 17, no. 5 (May/June 1998).
            http://www.sculpture.org/documents/scmag98/rdhunt/sm-rhunt.shtml

p. 52:   "as magical as using a brush . . ." Samella Lewis, *African American Art
            and Artists* (Berkeley: University of California Press), p. 323

p. 53:   "I'm like free jazz . . ." Polyxeni Potter, "Memory as Medicine"
            Emerging Infectious Diseases 18, no. 2 (February 2012), p. 363.

p. 58:   "Mr. Lawrence attempts to incorporate . . ." Michael Brenson,
            "Public Art at New Federal Building in Queens," *New York Times*
            (March 24, 1989), p. F-1.
            http://www.nytimes.com/1989/03/24/arts/review-art-public-art-at-new-
            federal-building-in-queens.html?pagewanted=all&src=pm

CHRONOLOGY

1876 Edward M. Bannister and Edmonia Lewis exhibit their work at the Centennial Exposition in Philadelphia.

1886 Jennie Smith discovers Harriet Powers's "Bible Quilt" at the Athens, Georgia, Cotton Fair.

1891 In an attempt to gain artistic acceptance, Henry O. Tanner leaves America and moves to Paris, France.

1920s African-American artists like Aaron Douglas and Augusta Savage thrive during the creative period known as the Harlem Renaissance.

1945 Jackie Ormes's comic strip *Patti-Jo 'n' Ginger* begins an 11-year run in the *Pittsburgh Courier*, a newspaper for African Americans.

1948 Photographer Gordon Parks becomes the first African American to work at *Life* magazine.

1949 Dr. John T. Biggers starts the art department at Texas State University.

1960 Alma Thomas retires from teaching to focus on painting full time.

1971 The Museum of Modern Art in New York holds a major exhibition of Romare Bearden's work, titled "Prevalence of Ritual."

1988 Graffiti artist and painter Jean-Michel Basquiat dies at age 28.

1991 Faith Ringgold's first children's book, *Tar Beach*, wins the Coretta Scott King Award for Illustration.

2009 Richard Hunt receives a Lifetime Achievement Award from the International Sculpture Center.

2011 A fourth season of Aaron McGruder's *The Boondocks* airs on the Cartoon Network.

2012 Radcliffe Bailey's show "Memory as Medicine" is displayed in San Antonio, Texas.

Of the Jacob Lawrence mosaic "Community," a *New York Times* art critic wrote, "Mr. Lawrence attempts to incorporate the colors and energy of the streets around the building into a tough, vibrant statement of physical labor and collective effort."

GLOSSARY

centennial—a celebration to mark the 100th anniversary of something.

collage—a picture made by sticking cloth, pieces of paper, photographs, and other objects onto a surface.

exhibit—to show in public.

fellowship—money awarded to a student for advanced studies.

harvest—crops gathered by farmers.

illustrated—shown in pictures.

inquisitive—questioning.

medallion—a medal or decoration.

migration—the act of moving from one place to another.

original—something that is new or unique.

pastoral—involving the countryside or farms.

professional—someone who earns money for the work they do.

regiment—a group of soldiers.

renaissance—a rebirth or revival of a culture.

segregation—the act of separating people based on race, gender, or other characteristics.

FURTHER READING

Duggleby, John. *Story Painter: The Life of Jacob Lawrence*. San Francisco: Chronicle Books, 1998.

Lawrence, Jacob. *The Great Migration: An American Story*. New York: HarperCollins, 1993.

Lyons, Mary E. *Starting Home: The Story of Horace Pippin, Painter*. New York: Atheneum, 1993.

———. *Stitching Stars: The Story Quilts of Harriet Powers*. New York: Aladdin, 1997.

Schroeder, Alan. *In Her Hands: The Story of Sculptor Augusta Savage*. New York: Lee & Low, 2009.

Schwartzman, Myron. *Romare Bearden: Celebrating the Victory*. New York: Franklin Watts, 1999.

INTERNET RESOURCES

http://americanhistory.si.edu/collections/object.cfm?key=35&objkey=7233& gkey=169

At the National Museum of American History's website, you can read about Harriet Powers's "Bible Quilt" and view larger images of some of its panels.

http://www.jackieormes.com/

This website describes a book written by Nancy Goldstein about Jackie Ormes, the first African-American woman cartoonist. The website offers a brief description of Ormes's life as well the chance to view some of her most famous comic strips.

http://www.faithringgold.com/

Faith Ringgold's website offers a biography written by the artist and writer, a list of books she has written and projects she is working on, a FAQ section, and links to online images of her work.

http://www.nga.gov/kids/zone/beardencg.pdf

The website of the National Gallery of Art in Washington D.C. provides a young people's guide to an exhibition of the life and art of Romare Bearden.

http://whitney.org/www/jacoblawrence/meet/lifes_work.html

The Whitney Museum website offers biographical information about Jacob Lawrence and many examples of his paintings.

INDEX

Numbers in **bold italics** refer to captions.

CONTRIBUTORS

CAROL ELLIS has written several books for young people. Her subjects have included law in Ancient Greece, the Gilded Age, endangered species, and martial arts. She lives in New York.

Senior Consulting Editor **DR. MARC LAMONT HILL** is one of the leading hip-hop generation intellectuals in the country. Dr. Hill has lectured widely and provides regular commentary for media outlets like NPR, the *Washington Post*, *Essence Magazine*, the *New York Times*, CNN, MSNBC, and *The O'Reilly Factor*. He is the host of the nationally syndicated television show *Our World With Black Enterprise*. Dr. Hill is a columnist and editor-at-large for the *Philadelphia Daily News*. His books include the award-winning *Beats, Rhymes, and Classroom Life: Hip-Hop Pedagogy and the Politics of Identity* (2009).

Since 2009 Dr. Hill has been on the faculty of Columbia University as Associate Professor of Education at Teachers College. He holds an affiliated faculty appointment in African American Studies at the Institute for Research in African American Studies at Columbia University.

Since his days as a youth in Philadelphia, Dr. Hill has been a social justice activist and organizer. He is a founding board member of My5th, a non-profit organization devoted to educating youth about their legal rights and responsibilities. He is also a board member and organizer of the Philadelphia Student Union. Dr. Hill also works closely with the ACLU Drug Reform Project, focusing on drug informant policy. In addition to his political work, Dr. Hill continues to work directly with African American and Latino youth.

In 2005, *Ebony* named Dr. Hill one of America's 100 most influential Black leaders. The magazine had previously named him one of America's top 30 Black leaders under 30 years old.